WORLD OF SPORTS

DEEP-SEA FISHING

Published by Smart Apple Media
123 South Broad Street, Mankato, Minnesota 56001

Photography: cover—CORBIS/Annie Griffiths Belt;
pages 4–5, 16–17, 20–21, 25–27, 30—CORBIS/Tony Arruza;
page 7—CORBIS; page 8—CORBIS/Jonathan Blair;
page 12—Bettmann/CORBIS; page 13—CORBIS/Bill Howes,
Frank Lane Picture Agency; pages 22–23, 31—CORBIS/Jef-
frey L. Rotman; page 19—ALLSPORT/Scott Halleran

Design and Production by EvansDay Design

LIBRARY OF CONGRESS CATALOGING-IN-PUBLICATION DATA

Vander Hook, Sue.
Deep-sea fishing / by Sue Vander Hook.
p. cm. — (World of sports)
Includes index.
Summary: Details the techniques and equipment of deep-
sea fishing, as well as the kinds of fish normally captured.
ISBN 1-887068-54-6
1. Deep-sea fishing—Juvenile literature. [1. Deep-sea fish-
ing. 2. Fishing.] I. Title. II. Series: World of sports
(Mankato, Minn.)
SH457.5.V35          2000
799.1'66—dc21          98-30292

First edition

9  8  7  6  5  4  3  2  1

# DEEP-SEA FISHING

SUE VANDER HOOK

*The line rose slowly and steadily and then the surface of the ocean bulged ahead of the boat and the fish came out. He came out unendingly and water poured from his sides. He was bright in the sun and his head and back were dark purple and in the sun the stripes on his sides showed wide and a light lavender. His sword was as long as a baseball bat and tapered like a rapier and he rose his full length from the water and then re-entered it, smoothly, like a diver and the old man saw the great scythe-blade of his tail go under and the line commenced to race out.*

The Old Man and the Sea

*by Ernest Hemingway*

# The Thrill of the Catch

**T**HE **ANGLER** SPOTS the huge bill of a fish jutting out of the water, and his adrenaline surges. First, the enormous fish leaps gracefully into the air. Then it arches its body and falls back into the water, showing off a broad tail that pounds the sea. Its perfectly pointed **dorsal fin** stands high on its back, confirming that the fish is a blue marlin, distinct from white marlins with their rounded fins.

*With more than 35 years of experience, captain Elly Brown takes up to six anglers offshore from Jupiter, Florida, in the 37-foot (11 m) Merritt. The biggest catch from this boat was a 1,003-pound (455 kg) bluefin tuna.*

The angler's fishing line screams from the **reel** in a blur. As the magnificent fish takes the bait, the hook is set, and the competition begins between the fish and the angler. The one with superior strategy, strength, and stamina will win.

The mighty fish charges to the right, then begins to dart away from the boat. Wearing a special belt to hold the end of the rod in place, the angler strains against the pull of the huge marlin. The fish has already used up three-fourths of the line on the big reel, and the line continues

to spool out. The angler shouts to his partner, telling him to turn the boat around. They must chase the fish to regain some fishing line. The angler reels line in as quickly as possible. For a while, the boat and the fish are side by side, moving at the same speed.

Suddenly, the fish rushes the boat, forcing the captain to angle the boat away. The infuriated marlin chases the boat and begins to gain on it, but then turns sharply, ripping yards of line off the reel once more.

Again, the fish runs while the angler chases it and reclaims line. Then the fish suddenly changes tactics, jumping out of the water and making a u-turn in mid-air. The great marlin screams through the water toward the front of the boat like a torpedo. The fishing line, full of **slack**, becomes a huge, looping arc in the air. The angler reels it in frantically.

The boat again runs with the fish, barely able to keep up with its speed of 40 miles (64 km) per hour. The marlin turns to the right, pulling more line off the reel. The fish **sounds**, diving straight down. It surfaces, then sounds again, this time with less force

**angler** *any person who fishes using a hook and a line*

**dorsal fin** *a large fin on a fish's back*

**reel** *a revolving device attached to a fishing rod and used to control the amount of fishing line in the water*

**slack** *looseness, especially in a line or rope*

**sound** *to plunge downward into deeper water*

and speed. The marlin tires with each run, and the angler's arms ache from holding the bending rod and cranking line back onto the reel.

*Captains Craig Ziegler and Rob Paquette won the 1997 Ocean City White Marlin Tournament in Maryland for the heaviest blue marlin—691 pounds (314 kg)—in the tournament.*

After several hours of competition, the fish and the angler are both exhausted. But the fish wears out first, finally rolling onto its side next to the boat, bright with angry blue stripes.

As the angler grabs the long bill of the mighty fish, the marlin makes one last effort to escape. The fish twists and turns violently in the water, slapping its tail on the surface in a frenzy of splashing. The commotion bolts the startled angler backward. The fish makes a final run, stopping 75 yards (68.6 m) from the boat, at last too weary to fight. Slowly, the angler reels in the marlin.

When the majestic fish again lies next to the boat, the angler places a tag near its dorsal fin and cuts the fishing line. The boat's captain takes pictures of the conquered fish and the proud angler. The fishermen decide that the beautiful marlin weighs at least 500 pounds (227 kg).

The fatigued but smiling angler takes one long, last look at the fish as if to say, "Nice game!" With a few sharp slaps of its tail, the mighty marlin disappears into the depths of the sea. The only reminders of the battle are the tag, the photographs, and the angler's memories. Perhaps these two competitors will meet again someday. Next time, maybe the fish will win.

# *The Past*

■━━━━■

LONG BEFORE FISHING became a popular pastime, people around the world fished to feed themselves. Archaeologists have discovered ancient drawings on cave walls that show people pulling fish from the sea. Today, people still fish for food, with the results of commercial fishing available on grocery store shelves. But fishing has also become a popular sport for all ages. Fishing with a hook and line is called angling and can be done in freshwater lakes and rivers or in the vast waters of the oceans.

*In 1964, captain George Bransford brought in the first black marlin weighing more than 1,000 pounds (454 kg) to ever be caught off Australia's Great Barrier Reef between Cairns and Lizard Islands.*

Until a few hundred years ago, anglers caught fish using only a fishing line. The first lines were made of vines, braided grass, horsetail hairs, or silk. Anglers on the shore tied bait to the end of their lines and dangled it into the water as far out as their arms could reach.

To fish in deeper waters, anglers later attached their lines to long poles that were often nothing more than sticks. In the 1600s, anglers began putting a wire loop at the end of each pole. The line passed through the

hole, giving anglers greater control of their line and allowing them to **cast** the bait farther from the shore.

Fishing was not considered a sport until *The Compleat Angler* was published in 1653. This book contained the poetry, prose, and fish recipes of English writer Izaak Walton, who praised angling as a healthy and rewarding sport. Today's anglers still use many of the fishing techniques he described. His methods were so helpful that he has been called "the Father of Modern Fishing."

When anglers added hooks to their fishing lines, they found it much easier to catch fish. At first, they made hooks out of many different materials, including eagles' beaks, hawks' claws, wood, stone, bone, horns, and teeth. Bone hooks have been found that date back earlier than 5000 B.C.

**cast**  *to throw a fishing line into the water*

**barbs**  *sharp points extending backward from the main point of a fish hook*

**alloy**  *a substance formed of two or more metals*

**artificial fly**  *a combination of feathers, hair, floss, tinsel, and other materials tied to a hook to imitate an insect*

ENGLISH WRITER AND OUT-DOOR ENTHUSIAST IZAAK WALTON HELPED MAKE FISH-ING A POPULAR PASTIME WITH HIS 17TH-CENTURY BOOK THE COMPLEAT ANGLER.

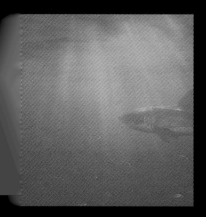

shank  *the part of a fishhook between the eye and the bend*

jigging  *a method of making jerking movements with a fishing line to lure fish*

corrode  *to eat away, usually through chemical action*

Today, thousands of varieties of fish hooks exist in many different sizes, shapes, and special designs. Most hooks have **barbs** that keep them from slipping out of fish's mouths. However, many sport anglers have begun using hooks without barbs, which can be removed easily.

Hooks today are made from carbon steel, stainless steel, or rustless **alloys**. Some are very thin so that **artificial flies** can be tied to them. Others are made of thick steel to catch big ocean fish. The type of hook that is used depends on the type of fish the angler is after. The wire size, **shank** length, hook size, and barb type all must be taken into consideration.

Nearly 200 years after Walton wrote his book, a spool, or "winder," was invented in Europe to hold extra fishing line. These clumsy, wooden devices attached to fishing poles were the very first reels.

*The all-tackle record for striped bass was broken on a moon-eclipsed night in 1981 when Bob Rochetta caught a 76-pound (34.5 kg) fish off the coast of Montauk, New York.*

Today, there are special reels available for every kind of fishing. Some reels are designed for casting, while others are better for **jigging**. The deep-sea angler uses strong, wide reels made of material that will not **corrode** or rust in saltwater. These reels are large enough to hold hundreds of yards of strong line that anglers need to catch huge, fast-running ocean fish. Anglers choose line carefully, making sure that it will not be easily cut by the sharp teeth or fins of a big fish. The line must also be heavy "test," able to withstand a lot of weight and steady force without breaking.

# The Able Angler

■──────■

**E**XPERIENCED ANGLERS KNOW how to search the waters for big fish. They often find large fish in areas where birds are hovering above the water. As the birds dive for smaller fish, an angler tries to catch the larger fish that have driven the smaller ones into a frenzy near the water's surface. Sometimes anglers find large fish near collections of seaweed or under small pieces of floating wood or debris.

*One of the first sailfish ever marked with a Billfish Foundation identification tag was caught and released on August 6, 1997, by a Loreto, Mexico, sportfishing fleet.*

In the Atlantic Ocean, game fish can often be found in the **Gulf Stream**.

A serious deep-sea angler uses a well-equipped boat large enough to navigate the open seas. An angler does not necessarily have to own the boat; he or she can rent a charter boat for half-day or full-day trips. The boat's captain supplies the appropriate **tackle** and bait. The charter boat is usually equipped with **outriggers**, heavy-duty rods, large reels, and 20- to 130-pound (9 to 59 kg) test line. The captain's experience with the cycle of tides, the migration of fish, and fish's feeding habits can

often lead an angler to a prize fish. An experienced captain can also coach an angler through a successful catch. Encouraging a less-experienced angler to let the fish run or jump freely at the appropriate times can prevent a snapped line. Keeping the fish from resting helps an angler to come out victorious in the end.

*For more than 20 years, captains Kirk Raymond and Barry Hitch have been guiding fishing charters off the coast of Jupiter, Florida. The biggest fish caught from their boat was a 900-pound (409 kg) tiger shark.*

**Surf casters** do not use boats at all. They fish during **high tide**, when sharks and other large fish approach the shore to feed on crabs, small fish, and eels. Surf casters try to catch these large predators as they feed. Using long, heavy-duty poles and strong lines, the anglers cast just beyond the crashing surf. When a fish is hooked, the angler reels it in close to shore, then uses a **gaff** to pull the fish up

**Gulf Stream** *the warm, powerful ocean current flowing northward along the east coast of North America*

**tackle** *equipment or gear used for fishing*

**outrigger** *a device attached to a boat to hold a fishing rod*

ATTEMPTING TO SHAKE LOOSE FROM AN ANGLER'S HOOK, A BEAUTIFUL BLUE MARLIN ERUPTS FROM THE SEA.

**surf casters** *anglers who try to catch large fish from the shore*

**high tide** *the rise of the waters of the ocean every 24 hours, caused by the gravitational attraction of the moon and the sun*

**gaff** *a big hook with a handle used to pull fish in to shore*

DEEP-SEA ANGLERS USUALLY FISH FROM LARGE BOATS THAT CAN MOVE ACROSS THE OCEAN QUICKLY AND HAVE PLENTY OF DECK SPACE.

onto the beach. Many large, powerful game fish have been caught from the shore.

Sport fishing can also be done in freshwater lakes and rivers, but anglers find the largest trophies of sport fishing in the deep, mysterious waters of the oceans. There, they battle huge fish that can weigh anywhere from 100 to 2,000 pounds (45–908 kg). These are the fish that captivate the world's most competitive anglers.

# The Mighty Fish

**O**F ALL THE SALTWATER game fish, billfish are the most impressive. When the long, sharp bill of a marlin, sailfish, or spearfish juts from the ocean's surface, even an experienced angler feels a rush of excitement.

Billfish are among the greatest of fighting fish. They are also outstanding leapers, so trying to catch one can be quite a thrill. Because billfish find their food near the surface of the water, anglers can spot them leaping and diving for their meals. Anglers often hook billfish

*The IGFA record for Atlantic blue marlin is 1,402 pounds (636.5 kg), and for Pacific, 1,376 pounds (625 kg). The Atlantic blue was caught off the coast of Brazil in 1992 by Paulo Amorim, and the Pacific blue was caught at Kaaiwi Point, Kona, Hawaii, in 1982 by Jay W. deBeaubien.*

with a technique called trolling. With a rod secured in an outrigger at the center of the boat, anglers release their baited lines behind the vessel. As the boat travels slowly through the water, anglers wait for a large fish to be drawn to the moving ballyhoo or mullet used as bait.

The blue marlin is the largest of the billfish; females reach weights in excess of 2,000 pounds (908 kg). With their huge, sail-like dorsal fin,

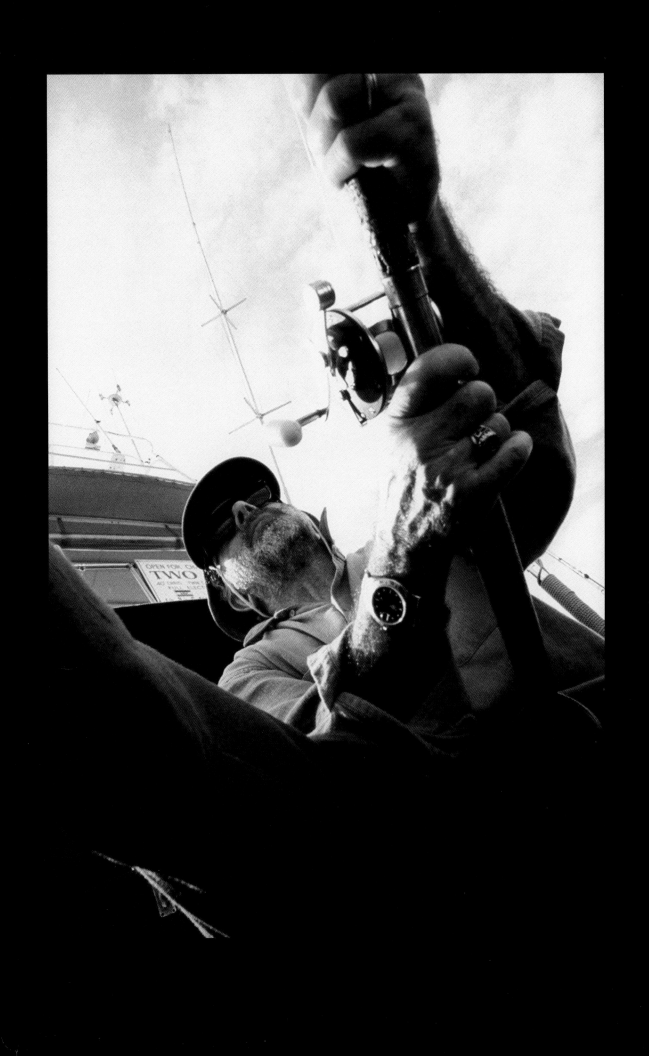

sailfish are one of the most unusual billfish. They are blue fish covered with black spots. Pacific sailfish, which are larger than those in the Atlantic, can weigh more than 200 pounds (91 kg). In the western North Atlantic Ocean, the United States government protects all billfish with a management plan that prohibits their commercial capture.

Billfish tournaments are popular competitions for sports anglers. Many anglers compete in the Bahamas Billfish Championship in April, May, and June. Other favorites are the White Marlin Open in Ocean City, Maryland, and the Big

Rock Blue Marlin Tournament in Moorehead City, North Carolina. Every year, anglers attempt to capture the largest fish and the tournament trophy. Some anglers at these tournaments may even break world records kept by the International Game Fishing Association (IGFA).

*Striped marlins have high, pointed dorsal fins and blue stripes. Found in the Pacific Ocean, they jump more than other marlin species. The IGFA record is a 494-pounder (224 kg) caught by Bill Boniface in 1986 in New Zealand.*

The swordfish also has a long bill, but it is from a different family of fish. Even years ago, when there were plenty of swordfish in the seas, these elusive giants were hard to catch. Today, they are a special prize for the able angler. Because swordfish meat is delicious, it carries a high price. Unfortunately, the swordfish population is decreasing every year due to the great demand for its meat.

The tuna belongs to the mackerel family. The largest of the tunas is the bluefin, which can weigh more than 2,000 pounds (908 kg). Catching a bluefin is one of the

migrate  to move from one region
to another, especially at certain
times of the year

spawning  depositing fish eggs or
producing young in great numbers

toughest struggles an angler will ever experience, because

the enormous fish will fight until it is totally exhausted. The

fish is so powerful that it often snaps fishing lines or tears

loose from the angler.

Unlike other fish, tuna are not entirely cold-blooded. Their

body temperatures can be significantly higher than the tem-

perature of the surrounding waters. According to Dr. Frank

Cary of the Woods Hole Oceanographic Institute in Massa-

chusetts, the tuna's higher body temperature triples the

muscle power of the fish, relative to

other fish of similar size.

Tuna have been known to **migrate**

great distances. They move south in the

fall and winter, **spawning** in the Gulf of

*Swordfish, the most
difficult angling prize
to catch, are found
worldwide at all
ocean depths. The
IGFA record is a 1,182-
pound (537 kg) fish
caught off of Chile in
1953 by L. Marron.*

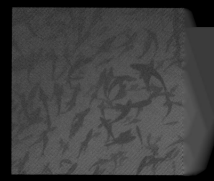

THE CREWMEN OF A COMMER-
CIAL FISHING BOAT USE
GAFFS TO PULL A BIG BLUEFIN
TUNA ABOARD. SUCH BLUEFIN
HARVESTS ARE CAREFULLY
REGULATED TODAY.

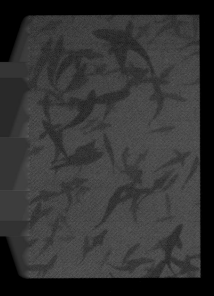

Mexico; in the spring, they migrate to northern waters from New Jersey to New-foundland. Bluefins are often found relatively close to shore in the summer, and anglers occasionally spot them in the shallow waters of Cape Cod Bay.

Overfishing has drastically reduced the number of tuna in the oceans. Governments have placed limits on the number of bluefin tuna—whose meat also brings a high price per pound—that can be caught each year. The status of the bluefin population is reviewed annually by the International Commission for the Conservation of Atlantic Tunas (ICCAT).

## *Rules of Fair Play*

**G**AME FISHING IS a sport with few written rules. However, anglers must obey laws that specify which fish can be caught and how many fish each angler can take. These laws help to ensure the survival of game fish species.

Anglers throughout the world are also participating in **catch-and-release** programs. In 1963, the Southwest Fisheries Science Center (SWFSC) in La Jolla, California, began its Billfish Tagging Program. The goal of the program is to help conserve and manage billfish numbers. Most North American anglers cooperate voluntarily by inserting a permanent tag near the dorsal fins of the billfish they catch. After a fish is released alive, it returns to its **habitat**. The angler fills out a billfish tagging report and mails it to the SWFSC. If another angler catches the fish and follows the same procedure, the SWFSC gains important information about the growth rate and migration patterns of that type of fish.

*Mako sharks are highly prized because they grow to more than 1,500 pounds (681 kg) and jump as high as 20 feet (6 m) when hooked.*

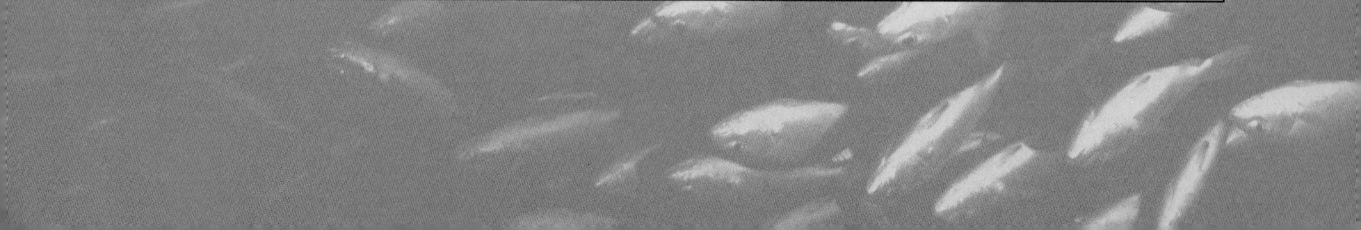

To promote the catch-and-release program, the IGFA allows anglers to weigh their catch in the boat and still qualify for a world record. The IGFA's Junior Angler World Record Program also allows for the catch, in-boat weighing, and release of record fish.

In 1997, Dr. Molly Lutcavage, a marine biologist from Boston's New England Aquarium, directed a research project on giant bluefin tuna. With the help of captain Ed "Cookie" Murray Jr. and his crew, Dr. Lutcavage spent four days tagging bluefin tuna weighing from 300 to 1,000 pounds (136 to 454 kg) with pop-up satellite tags. In the spring of 1998, the pop-up tags triggered their own time-

*The bluefin tuna, the largest tuna, is called the "greatest fighting fish in the world." The world record is a 1,496-pound (679 kg) giant caught near Nova Scotia in 1979 by Ken Fraser.*

**catch-and-release**  *the practice of letting fish go after they are caught*

**habitat**  *the natural environment of an animal*

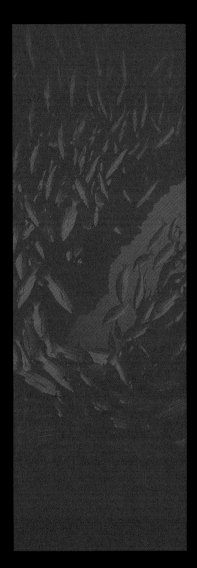

release, detached from the fish, and floated to the surface. A satellite uploaded information from the floating tags. Lutcavage then downloaded the satellite information to track the fish. Many sharks and marlins have also been outfitted with satellite tags.

Today's deep-sea anglers respect the oceans and the mighty fish that live there. Because of their **conservation** efforts, future anglers will be able to feel the pulse-quickening thrill of spotting a long bill in the dark seas. They will be able to appreciate the beauty of seeing a marlin leaping high in the air and to experience the satisfaction of outwitting the savvy sailfish—to know what it is like to conquer one of the majestic giants of the deep.

ALTHOUGH DEEP-SEA ANGLERS OFTEN USE ARTIFICIAL LURES TO CATCH BILLFISH, THEY MAY ALSO BAIT HOOKS WITH SMALL FISH SUCH AS MACKEREL.

# The Hunter or the Hunted

**IN A COMPETITION** between an angler and a big fish, it can be hard to figure out which one is the hunter. Large fish may charge the boat, and their powerful tails and sharp fins can injure anglers. But the ultimate challenge for a deep-sea angler is competing with a shark. Sharks can have up to five rows of extremely sharp teeth and weigh several tons. Long before the movie *Jaws* frightened swimmers from the water, people feared and hunted these giants of the sea.

*Frank Mundus has been called the "Monster Man" for his encounters with sharks. Since the 1950s, he has taken hundreds of people out on his charter boat,* Cricket II, *to fish for the giant predators.*

The great white shark has earned a reputation as a man-eater by occasionally attacking humans. Large white sharks prefer eating mammals to eating fish and are often found near seal populations around San Francisco and Maine. Out in deeper waters, white sharks will immediately attack an injured or dead whale, tearing it apart in amazing time. Skin divers and swimmers have been attacked by white sharks in the coastal waters off of California.

In 1986, captains Frank Mundus and Donnie Braddick used a rod and reel to catch a 3,427-pound (1,556 kg) white shark near Montauk, New York. However, their record catch was not recognized by the International Game Fishing Association, because the anglers used whale meat as bait—a practice that violates IGFA rules.

*The largest IGFA officially approved fish caught on a rod was a great white shark weighing 2,664 pounds (1,209.5 kg) by Alfred Dean in Australia in 1959.*

The mako shark, the white shark, and the **porbeagle** are among the great fighting sharks. The mako is very fast, grows to a large size, and can jump as high as 20 feet (6 m) when hooked. Makos often swim within a few miles of shore in the summer in search of bluefish, their favorite food. The official, **all-tackle** IGFA world record shark catch was a 1,115-pound (506 kg) mako caught in the Indian Ocean off of Mauritius in 1990.

**porbeagle** *a North Atlantic
shark with a pointed nose and
crescent-shaped tail*

**all-tackle** *fishing using rods,
reels, line, hooks, floats, and
sinkers*

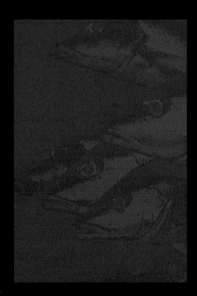

The danger posed by sharks may be exactly what makes anglers want to fish for these predators. It's a safari al-

*The longest recorded fight with a fish is 37 hours, by Bob Ploeger (U.S.) with a king salmon on July 12–13, 1989.*

most anyone can afford. Any angler who encounters one of the majestic ocean giants participates in a sport that matches wits, muscles, and seagoing skills with an unlikely opponent—a true monster of the deep.